**THIS IS AN UNOFFICIAL, UNAUTHORIZED, AND INDEPENDENT PARODY BOOK.**

Y0-DJP-799

PUBLISHED IN 2015 BY
RAZZBERRY BOOKS
EMAIL: INFO@RAZZBERRYBOOKS.COM

© 2015 RAZZBERRY BOOKS

ALL RIGHTS RESERVED.
NO PART OF THIS PUBLICATION MAY BE REPRODUCED, DISTRIBUTED,
OR TRANSMITTED IN ANY FORM OR BY ANY MEANS, INCLUDING
PHOTOCOPYING, RECORDING, OR OTHER ELECTRONIC OR MECHANICAL
METHODS, WITHOUT THE PRIOR WRITTEN PERMISSION OF THE PUBLISHER.

PRINTED IN THE UNITED STATES OF AMERICA

ISBN-13: 978-1512223477
ISBN-10: 1512223476

D1712052

# THE QUARTER QUELL IS UPON US.
## DRAW A LINE TO THE WEAPON EACH TRIBUTE WILL NEED TO PREVAIL AND JOIN THE REVOLUTION.

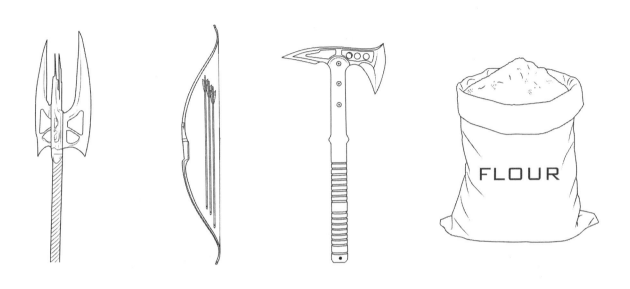

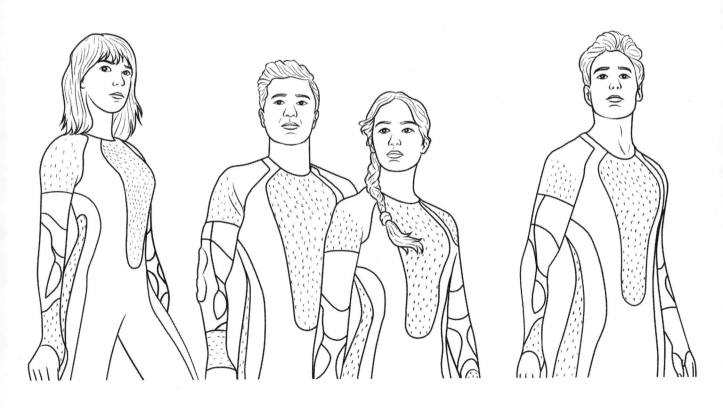

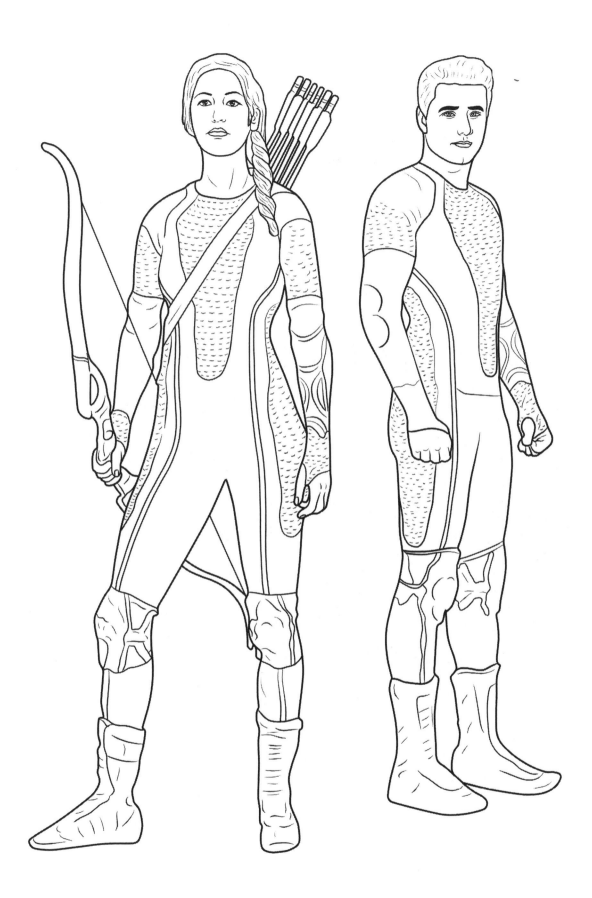

DRAW AND COLOR A DRESS FOR KATNISS
THAT SHE WON'T TRIP OVER AT THE OSCARS.

The Capitol has decided to do this year's reaping by wordsearch. Wow, that's a weird plot twist. The first five names you find will go to the Games.

```
Y Q L C A V S H R P R M Q J E
Y I K T L S C U A R H U E Z F
C Q E N I T W T C E Y O V B F
S E A N I V T Z H M B A E R I
P S T M B S Z B E N C F F B E
M A Y R V M S Y L I E O J G E
K A F E L P C O N A N N I C O
H F E L C T N O R D Y D K H A
N A L D U Q M K N I F Q G C E
G B T N B Z A Y Y U K F B M I
K T W A C T I O E B Y N U V M
Q G L H B I Q F O B S Q A J D
Y T A C N U T F J M B R J S N
A R C E S S Y O U G D L W C T
T Z X A L W C Q X I M H V E G
```

CHANDLER    KATNISS
CINNA        MONICA
EFFIE        PEETA
GAEL         PHOEBE
HAYMITCH    RACHEL
JOEY         ROSS

OH DEAR. SOMETHING IMPORTANT IS MISSING!
CONNECT THE DOTS TO HELP HAYMITCH OUT.

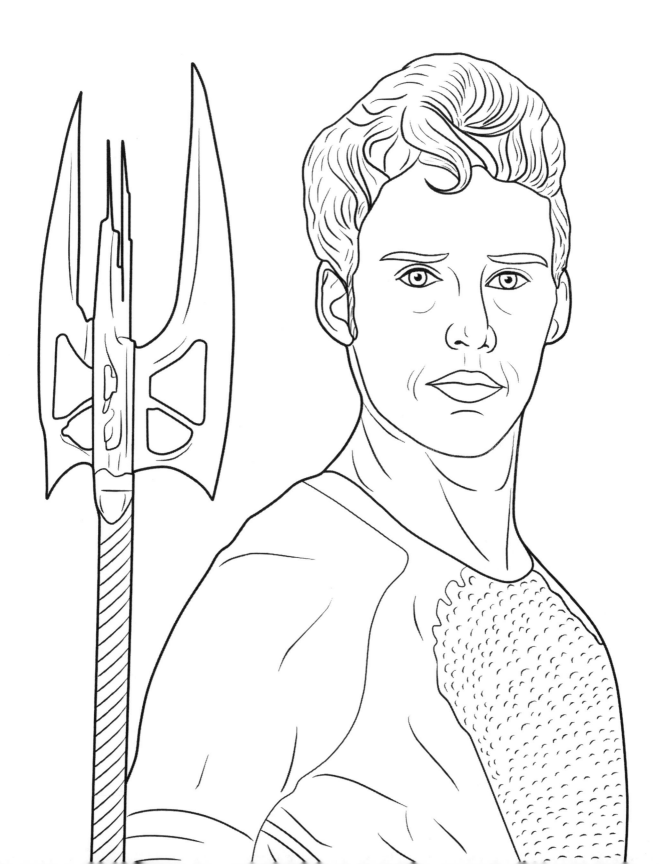

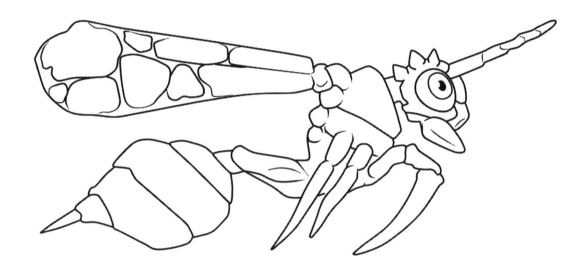

EFFIE HATES LOOKING DRAB. COLOR IN AND CUT OUT
SOME WIGS FOR ANOTHER "BIG! BIG DAY"!

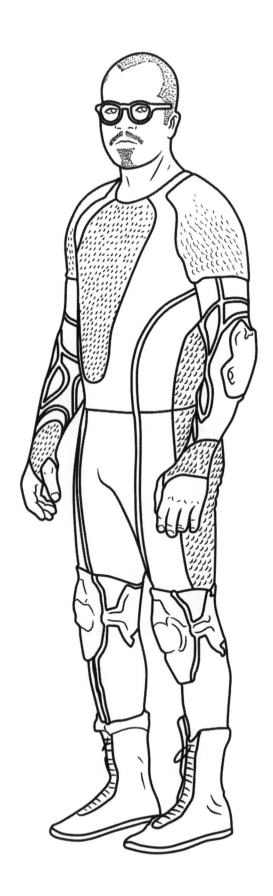

46882955R20024

Made in the USA
Lexington, KY
19 November 2015